WIZARDLY WIT & WISDOM

Copyright © 2020 Tracy Hermes

Book design and drawings by Gina Ylagan
Photo Credits: Louise Hanley

ISBN 978-1-7361748-0-7
ISBN 978-1-7361748-2-1
ISBN 979-8-5760789-3-6

Published by Soul Infusion, LLC Edwards, CO
Printed in the United States of America
www.wizardlywisdom.com

Dedicated to

MY KINNY-KIN-KIN

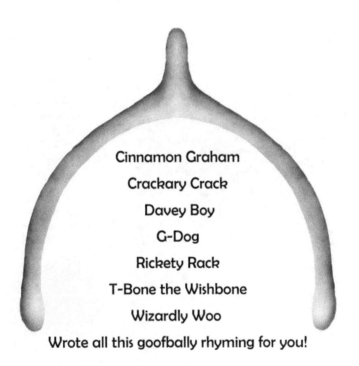

Cinnamon Graham

Crackary Crack

Davey Boy

G-Dog

Rickety Rack

T-Bone the Wishbone

Wizardly Woo

Wrote all this goofbally rhyming for you!

...and of course our little doodlebug too

WIZARDLY WIT & WISDOM

Deep thoughts, a laugh, maybe a blunder
Poems to make you giggle and wonder

Poems by Tracy Hermes

Drawings by Gina Ylagan

Acknowledgements

I would like to express my sincere gratitude to all those in my life that have loved, guided, and cheered me on in support of this book. This a project of the soul, of *my* soul, and I hope it inspires, ignites and infuses yours as well.

I have been blessed with an incredible family, circle of friends, and endless mentors along with inspiring leaders that have served as my muses. I would like to acknowledge my loving husband, Rick, who has always believed in me and has encouraged me to follow my heart and dreams; our boys, Zach and Davis, to whom I hope these messages land and offer guidance in their lives; Gina, for her incredible talent and patience with me throughout this entire process as we worked so hard creating this together; Taylor, for her graphic design skills and assistance in launching this project; Danette, for trusting and believing in me to work on her book which, in turn, inspired mine; and my heartfelt gratitude for EVERY person in my life that I have deep connections with...*you know who you are!* You have lifted me up, stood by my side and believed in me when I did not always believe in myself. I am profoundly grateful for my tribe.

The following is a list of wise leaders who have inspired some of my poems. I am humbled by each and every one of them and it is my hope and dream that we ALL continue sprinkling goodness upon the world.

JOEL OSTEEN inspired I AM, *p.10*

NICHOLE McELHANEY inspired THE MOON, *p.12*

LAO-TZU inspired MUDDY WATERS, *p.13;* THE ASCENT, *p.126*

DOROTHY LAW NOLTE inspired TEACH ME THE GOOD STUFF PLEASE, *p.24*

JIM ROHN inspired DON'T PAY THAT GUY, *p.27*

TONY ROBBINS inspired LUCKY CLOVER, *p.29;* SWITCH IT, CHANGE IT, REARRANGE IT, *p.136*

ALAN COHEN inspired YOU ARE YOU, *p.33*

AMY PURDY inspired WHO IS SHE? *p.40*

ROTARY CLUB inspired SERVICE ABOVE SELF, *p.42*

ANITA MOORJANI inspired ANITA, *p.60*

JACK CANFIELD inspired TRUST THE GPS, *p.62*

ADMIRAL WILLIAM H. McRAVEN inspired MAKE YOUR BED, *p.87*

SAM PARKER inspired ONE DEGREE SHIFT, *p.91*

JEAN-PAUL SARTRE inspired C WHAT HAPPENS, *p.106*

LOUISE HAY inspired HAY, YOU! *p.122*

JIM KWIK inspired KWIK INSIGHT, *p.123*

WILLIAM ARTHUR WARD inspired RISKY BUSINESS, *p.129*

WAYNE DYER inspired ORANGE YOU GLAD I DIDN'T SAY BANANA, *p.134*

The following are old stories retold in my own creative way, all of which have inspired and helped me on my journey. I am thankful for the wonderful messages they convey.

TWO WOLVES, *p.2;* GOLDEN BUDDHA, *p.4;* ROCKY, *p.6;* THE STRUGGLE IS REAL, *p.64;* THE FOREST OF TRUTH, *p.69;* THE TENTH APPLE, *p.96;* THE RISE, *p.103;* THE PEAR TREE, *p.105;* TIME WILL TELL, *p.108*

LET US KEEP PASSING ALONG ALL OF LIFE'S BEAUTIFUL MESSAGES AND STORIES…WE MAY NEVER KNOW HOW THEY MAY BRIGHTEN A DAY OR BRING HOPE WHERE THERE WAS NONE.

JOIN ME IN SPREADING THE LOVE!

Acknowledgements

x

Table of Contents

Table of Contents

THE NAKED TRUTH

The truth is hard to hear
It can bring up hurt and fear
It's time to reflect
On truths we neglect
Questioning beliefs that we endear

So that you won't mishear
Truth is dressed up with cashmere
Soft and warm with glory
In rhyme or a story
So the message lands crystal clear

Things aren't always as they appear
Challenge your story to persevere
It's time to retreat
With these gifts so sweet
Naked Truth dressed for the new frontier!

Enjoy, my dear

♡ Tracy

Once upon a time
There was an old Cherokee
He told his young grandson
There's a fight inside of me

Inside me lives two wolves
And they have a lot of strife
Yet these same two fighting wolves
Have taught me how to live my life

They fight with one another
Morning, noon and night
Sometimes it's really hard to say
Who's wrong and who is right

The one wolf, he is evil
He is anger
Sorrow and greed
He lies a lot
Resents a bunch
He's arrogant indeed

The other wolf is hope and love
Not evil
He is good
He's peace and joy
Kind and true
And does everything he should

The old Cherokee continued
It also lives in you
The very fight between these wolves
Lives in EVERY person, too!

The grandson thought about it
For some time
And asked which wolf will win
He simply replied
The one you feed
And left him with a grin

So then he knew
To choose the good
It's he who guides the voice
The life he truly
Wants to live
Depends upon this choice!

I AM...

Whatever follows the words
"I AM"
Will always come looking for you

Don't be afraid or act surprised
Like it jumped out and just said BOO!

If you say
"I AM"
Happy

Then Happy you shall be

You then will find the reasons to be Happy - you will see!

SO PLEASE watch your words
Especially these simple two

Whatever comes after the words
"I AM"
Will always come looking for you!

Perfectly

Imperfect

Stop trying to be perfect

It will never be

I wasn't meant to be perfect

Just perfectly me

It's ok to make ~~miss steaks~~ mistakes

And learn from my dismay

I then will have more character

And Strength to display

GOLDEN

In 1957
On a very special day
A giant golden Buddha
Was uncovered from the clay

Hidden from glory for two hundred years
The clay that did conceal
Exposed this gem to our wonderment
And became the great reveal

When the Burmese army
Invaded Siam
Two centuries before
The Siamese monks
Swore to protect
This shrine they did adore

The golden Buddha was covered
Twelve inches thick with clay
When the Burmese army passed it by
No attention did they pay

All the monks were killed in war
Yet the Buddha so divine
Stayed hidden in it's clay disguise
As a cheap village shrine

Construction of a road then forced
A monastery to relocate
Along with the Buddha statue
That stood tall and clay ornate

The crane tried to lift the statue
But due to the tremendous
Weight it bore
It started to crack
They lowered it down
Gently to the floor

This caused the monk to worry
Then rain had started to fall
They quickly covered with a tarp
And had to suspend the haul

BUDDHA

He went back out to check on it
In the middle of the night
He peeked his head up under the tarp
To see it with his light...

...And much to his delight
...He saw a shimmer that was bright
...Grabbed a chisel and a hammer
...To now expose more of the site

As he knocked off shards of clay
The gleam grew much much bigger
He couldn't believe
What stood before him
A glorious solid gold figure!

And just like you
That beautiful light
Has been there all along
It was never lost
Just covered in clay
Of which it didn't belong

Please never forget the glory you are
And shine your golden light
Peel back layers to expose your truth
And shine with all your might

THE
MOON

I felt lost
I felt low
Inside my head
Spun like a twister

I looked up
I looked down
When I heard
This little whisper

I glanced up
Saw her light
It was the moon
So divine

My darling
The moon said to me...

...You don't have to be whole to shine

MUDDY
WATERS

DO YOU HAVE THE

PATIENCE

TO JUST SIT BACK AND WAIT

'TIL THE MUD SETTLES

AND THE WATER IS CLEAR

WHEN THINGS DON'T FEEL SO GREAT?

CAN YOU REMAIN UNMOVING

'TIL THE RIGHT ACTION BECOMES KNOWN?

THEN YOU WON'T BE STRESSING

AND WITH

FAITH

YOU WILL BE SHOWN

R
O
C
K

Y

A professional boxer knows how winning is done
Here is a message one gives to his son

ROCKY BALBOA
His words ring true
There on the screen as if speaking to you

He tells his son - *Here's something you must know*
Life's not just rainbows - It can give a hard blow

It can be MEAN
It can be NASTY
No matter how tough you are
It can beat you right down to your knees
And even leave a scar

Don't let it keep you down
GET BACK UP *if you shall fall*
But if it does you must ***RISE UP***
And then you must ***STAND TALL!***

Fight for what you really want
For in that there is no shame
You must be willing to take some hits
And no one should you blame

A coward points the finger...
At him...
And her...
And that...
But you my boy this is not you
You must step up to bat!

BELIEVE IN YOURSELF
It is a must!
If you don't then who else will?
This lesson is huge
Can change your life
If you choose not to sit still

Don't care what others think
It's <u>your</u> job to fill your cup
NEVER EVER
Point the finger
And when you're hit
YOU GET BACK UP!

This my son
Is how winning is done
KEEP YOUR HEAD UP
With your face to the sun

BAMBOO

I'll be like bamboo

This I do vow

The higher I grow

The deeper I'll bow

12

HMMM...

Something to ponder

Something to wonder

What if there's a gift

From all of life's thunder?

...look for life's rainbows

Corona...

Corona
Corona
I just wanna moan-a
I'm tired of being here stuck in my home-a

I miss-a my school
I miss-a my friends
I just wish-a this whole stupid thing would just end

I just want to roam-a
Or get my diploma
Or go to the playground
With sis or alone-a

Don't get me wrong-a
I love mom and dad
But they also miss
The old life that they had

Sometimes I'm happy
Sometimes I'm sad
I like sleeping later
And seeing my dad

School work is easy
I do it real fast
I miss the old days
Please be over alas

Corona...

Corona
Corona
I'll never again moan-a
Because I've been shown-a
A whole different way

I appreciate things
That I never did before
And maybe that's the reason
It showed up at our door

I know there's a blessing
If you look then you'll see
It's just hard being inside
When at school I should be

Oh CORONA
CORONA
JUST LEAVE US ALONE-A
WE'RE READY TO GET OUT
OF THESE WALLS OF OUR HOME-A!

Bye bye...go on....Yup that's right...time to go away...
yup that's what you heard me say, Now...go... go...GO ON

WISHES

&

MAGIC
TRICKS

Mom says due to quarantini
She won't fit in her bikini

Burritos
Bellini
Snack
Panini
Burgers
French fries
Hot dog weenie

It's not so good for self-esteem-y
I should be eating more zucchini

We were supposed to go to Santorini
But now because of quarantini
That won't happen without Houdini

Or 3 wishes to a genie

So I guess for now it's FETTUCCINE!

LONGEST.   MONTH.   EVER.

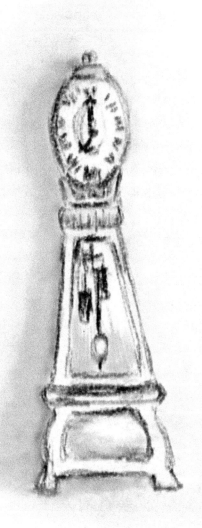

Tick tock goes the clock

Here we go again

Keep away

Six feet they say

Will this ever end?

OH HOW I MISS...

Climbing a tree
Skinning my knee
Even my best friend who's picking on me
Her name is Leigh
She's English you see
She eats little sandwiches while sipping on tea
The buzz of a bee
My bike lock and it's key
The big white teepee
Off the trail by the tree
Not just saying "me"
A group I call "we"
Karate gi
And
Friends sparring with me
A day to go ski
The ocean or sea
A fun shopping spree
With friends, one, two or three
Soon we will be
Glove and mask free
Biggest bright smiles
We ever did see!

Yippee!

(Now hurry up)

BOOBTUBE

boob tube (n.) *slang for television set*

TEL-E-VISION
Don't tell me
"TELL-A-VISION"
Comes from me

I get to choose
What I choose to see
Who I am
And what I'll be

You try and say what I should hear
But I get to say what goes in my ear!

I am the boss of me!
Even if we disagree!
I will use my mind
Not let my mind use me!

I'M A CRITICAL THINKER
GOOD NEWS DRINKER
SILLY LITTLE STINKER
THAT IS ME!

Just like the painter with his brush
Paints his first and last brush stroke
I'll pave my own way NOW
And I'll do this 'til I croak!

(so there!)

SHAKY EGG

She tried to sing
She tried to dance
But neither did she stand a chance

She tried guitar
She was subpar
How could she be a superstar?

She racked her brain
What could she do?
A musical path she must pursue

Make music with her feet
Now that's a thought!
So on to tap, what fun it brought!

Nope, that wasn't it
The search continued
Then one fine day she met this dude

"Come up on stage
And shake this egg
My guy can't play - he broke his leg"

She soon would find
Where her dreams land
On stage - huge crowd - shaky egg in hand

She started to get noticed
Wherever she'd go
"There's the girl with the egg, she should have her own show!"

She never gave up
And that's a fact
Now she's living out her dream with a solo act!

ROUND & ROUND & ROUND

These thoughts, they keep running around in my head. I wish they would stop, I want peace instead...

23

TEACH ME
THE GOOD STUFF PLEASE

If criticized I'll learn to condemn

If things are hostile I'll learn to fight

If ridiculed and mocked

I'll be shy and stay out of sight

I'll always feel guilty

If I live with shame

But I'll learn patience

If tolerance is the aim

I'll learn confidence through encouragement

Self-esteem through praise and nourishment

I will learn about justice

If I live with being fair

And will learn to have faith

When I feel safe in your care

I'll learn to really like myself

As approval is unfurled

With friendship, acceptance and love for myself

I will learn to find love in the world

TRUST

T
R
U
S
T

T
R
U
S
T

TRUST

If you don't know
Let it go
Answers will come soon

GLOWSTICK

We're kind of like a glowstick glowing in the night

Sometimes we have to break first

So we can shine real bright

DON'T PAY THAT GUY

You can't pay someone to do push-ups for you
You gotta take pride in yourself and everything you do

You gotta do it for yourself
You can't go run and hide
When it's you who did the work
You'll be beaming with pride

So step up and work hard
Hold your head up high
The push-ups feel much better than if you tried to pay that guy

(pssst...don't pay that guy!)

THE GREAT COMEBACK

Zig Ziggy Ziggidy Zach
Went for a walk on the railroad track
He said he didn't know when he'd be back
He had all he needed in his giant backpack

Zig Ziggy Ziggidy Zach
Didn't understand it's not all on your back
The lessons that happen some say we attract
He learned to work hard and it's no good to slack

Zig Ziggy Ziggidy Zach
Now had more lessons that were more abstract
He paced up and down on that railroad track
Fighting bad thoughts that he could not attack

Zig Ziggy Ziggidy Zach
Found a great role model having his back
He uncovered some truths - and also - in fact...
He took off the monkey which weighed on his back

Zig Ziggy Ziggidy Zach
Through love and acceptance had nothing of lack
Grateful and humbled as burdens unpack
This here's the story…Ziggidy Zach's great comeback!

LUCKY CLOVER

LIVE LUCKY

BE A BLESSING

TO EVERY PERSON

YOU'RE ADDRESSING

UH-OH

My hair was long
It looked so cool
But then one day
It did not rule
My friend was bored
And took my mop
And decided just to
Shave the top

I now look weird
It makes me laugh
I wish I were
A tall giraffe
The top of my head
You would not see
No one would know
Except for me

SEE I TOLD YA

I'm so good at sleeping I can do it with my eyes closed

And just then

I dozed

z z Z

YOU ARE YOU

Stop looking for answers outside of you

You have all the answers *(you are the guru)*

They have always been inside of you

That is why it is spelled

GEE - YOU ARE YOU

GURU

MY TWO CENTS

The guy by the fence

Is acting real dense

He's really intense

And doesn't make sense...

It's at my expense

If I try and make sense

'Cause there is no defense

And you can't make sense

From nonsense

Isn't this common sense, hence the intense sense of his pretense?

His immense dispense of offense is pure nonsense

So don't even try to make sense

Here is my pence

There, now you have my two cents

Stop the suspense and just use common sense!

"YOU TALKIN' TO ME?"

The difference between *listen* and *hear*
Is *hear* just goes right out the ear

In one ear
Out the other
If busted
Then punished
By your mother

Respect is when you <u>truly</u> *listen*
A skill to polish to make you glisten

MANNERS

Please and **thank you**
Hold the door
Don't stop there
There's so much more

A **Firm handshake**
When you greet
Look them in the eyes
'Til both eyes meet

When they say
Hey kid - how do you do?
Answer first
Then ask them too

Listen to what
They have to say
Stay and **talk**
No time for play

Once you're done
You say **farewell**
GOOD MANNERS
WILL ALWAYS SERVE YOU WELL!

Thank you, farewell...now you can play

WHAT A JOKE

When I tell this joke it really feels like a sin…

"See that cemetery? People are dying to get in!"

DON'T STOP

Before answers
Come **QUESTIONS**

Always

ASK
ASK
ASK

You'll be so much brighter
Prepare for the task

Inquisitive
Much more to give
Curiosity
Expand

Your mind has more clarity
When this you demand

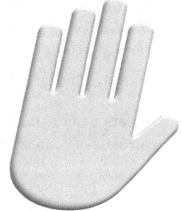

Fill me up buttercup
I want to know all

QUESTIONS
ASK
QUESTIONS

For once and for all

WHO IS SHE?

Oh my friend
You're so Purdy
How'd you get those
Legs so sturdy?

You went dancing with a star
Now the world knows who you are

You're on your own two feet
As a challenged athlete

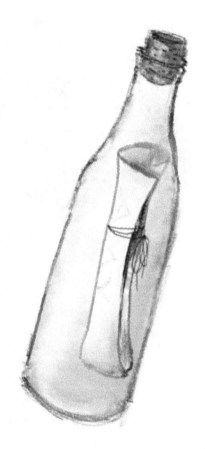

As you snowboard
Quite the feat
And adversity defeat

I hold your story dear
Choosing courage over fear
Never giving up
You always persevere

You are a hero and a model
You always push the throttle

Use the hints to figure out this message in a bottle!

WANNA BET?

When would
NOW
Be a good time
To step into

Your dream?

With
COURAGE
And
FAITH
You will see
It's not as hard
As it may seem

NOW
GET ON UP
AND START TODAY

I'll even make a bet

That if you

GET ON IT
And start right NOW
You WILL NOT have regret!

SERVICE
ABOVE
SELF

The Rotary Club
Has a moral code
Of honor
And respect

I found a coin
With their 4-way test
Great questions
To detect

Is it the truth?
Is it fair to all?

Building goodwill
And friendships
That stand tall?

Is it beneficial
To all
Concerned?

Great questions
Here
To be discerned

Now read those again
Oh how I wish
That everybody knew

To ask these questions
In all we think
And all we say and do!

The world would be a better place

MS. P.

Every time I see
Ms. P.
She makes me look
Inside of me

She makes me jump
On the trampoline
And love myself
Be nice not mean

She makes me say
Three things I love
About myself
To rise above

Then 3 more things
I'm grateful for
Right. When. I. Walk.
In. The. Door.

So annoyed at first
I just want to play
So please Ms. P.
JUST GO AWAY!

But now I see
I DO love me
And all because
SHE MADE ME SEE!

(Thanks Ms. P…grateful I'll always be!)

Every day
These words
I say
And
Write them
In a
Book

Even If
They
Don't
Feel true
I'll
Speak them
'Til they took

Affirming
Who I
Want to
Be
As if
Already
True

Have patience
And you
Won't believe
The change
You'll
See
In you!

FAKE

'TIL

MAKE

IT

YOU

IT

I AM ♡

I am
COURAGE
I am
FAITH
I am
GUIDED FROM ABOVE

I am
JOY
I am
PEACE
I am
SURRENDER
and I'm
LOVE

I am
TRUST
I am
ABUNDANCE
I am
BEAUTY
I am
GRACE

What words
Can you
Begin
To say
That you
Should
NOW
Embrace?

LET IT GO

Are you fighting too hard for something?

Maybe it's not meant to be

Perhaps you're better off without it

Let it go and set it free

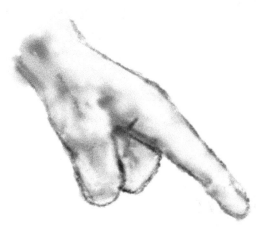

BACK ATCHA!

WHENEVER YOU BLAME AND POINT THE FINGER

THERE'S THREE FINGERS POINTING BACK

FIND YOUR PART

NO MATTER HOW SMALL

LOOK WITHIN AND DON'T ATTACK

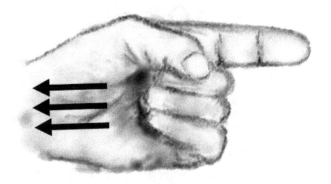

YOU CHOOSE

Sometimes you have to ask yourself
Right
Smack
In the middle
Of a fight
Which would I rather choose right now

To be
HAPPY
OR

to be
RIGHT?

Swallow your pride, get over yourself and choose happy!

EMPTY CUP

Pain can leave an empty hole

Like something's missing in your soul

But what matters is how you fill that space

Nurture it with love and grace

(It's the emptiness of a cup that makes it useful)

I SCREAM

Mom says be really careful
WHAT YOU FOCUS ON EXPANDS
Watch where you put your energy
'Cause where it goes it lands

This got me REALLY excited
It actually felt like a dream
Now all of my focus and energy
Went to my very favorite ice cream

I thought about
Rocky Road
Every. Second. Of. The. Day.
Will FOCUS bring
A giant bowl
If I push other
Thoughts away?

After dinner
I sat and waited
Anticipation filled my soul

But mom just
Gave me an apple
Instead of a
Giant ice cream bowl

Wait what?

I'm not giving up...
FOCUS
You got this
She said it herself...

What you focus on expands!

"I SCREAM
YOU SCREAM
WE ALL SCREAM FOR ICE CREAM!
I SCREAM
YOU SCREAM
WE ALL SCREAM FOR ICE CREAM!
I SCREAM
YOU SCREAM
WE ALL SCREAM FOR ICE CREAM!"

And out it came

THE **BIGGEST** BOWL
Of ice cream
You ever did see

Lucky
Lucky
Lucky me

Maybe she just wanted me
To stop this "scream for ice cream"
Or maybe
It was my **FOCUS**
That expanded my biggest dream!

Who knows, but I'm happy either way
Maybe I'll learn this lesson some other day

For now I just need to loosen my belt
and eat my ice cream so it does not melt ;)

Gag me with a spoon

Like
Gross me out the door

Like
Totally

Like
Oh my God

Like
We are hot for sure!

THE *LIKE* EPIDEMIC

The, *like, excessive use of this word*
Makes you sound unsure when at the "mike"
Or, *like, everyday speech, rather than pause*
You fill the space with a word like, *like...(which i so dislike)*

This started in the 1970's
With, *like, the funny little "valley girl" speak*
Like, in every sentence
Like, these valley girls they would sneak

It's still misused and overused
I'm begging you, please, *like, tweak*
Like, it makes you sound uneducated
And your grammar, *like, seems so weak*

So, *like, be aware of this poor choice*
Of *like, saying like, like, rather than pause*
Say nothing at all, not even um or er
And help me try and fight this cause!

WISHFUL

DOMO ARIGATO

Is my motto

Not just a song

By Mr. Roboto

DOMO ARIGATO

Things already

You have got-o

Don't forget

To ARIGATO

Wishes

That you really want-o

DOMO ARIGATO

Little things like

My gelato

Even just for

Sipping tea

While eating

My biscotto

THANKING

DOMO ARIGATO
For the state of
Colorado
And even for
The penny found
Lying
In the grotto

DOMO ARIGATO
Winning ticket
In the lotto
My multi-million
Dollar win
From hitting
The jackpot-o!

DOMO ARIGATO
How I love
This motto
Now and later
Giving thanks
DOMO ARIGATO

THREE STICKS

I thought this was funny
I thought this was cute
From fancy to silly
It's really a hoot

William Arthur the third
After his name was three lines
Representing a three
So the line was three times

He then got the nickname
From guys and the chicks
Not William no more
He's now **Billy - Three - Sticks!**

William Arthur III

STUPOR-FREE

I heard a very wise thing from Mrs. Cooper

"Show me your friends and I'll show you your future"

I better get me some friends that are really SUPER

Not worrying about looking like a big party pooper

I want a super duper future Mrs. Cooper

So off I'll go and I'll be a storm trooper

Live my life with intention and not in a stupor

Making you proud 'cause my friends are so super

Which helps me create a really great future

Thanks again Mrs. Cooper

You sure are super!

FR END
GARDEN

Bad choice of friends

Can supersede

Wishes dreams

And virtuous creed

I must step in

And take the lead

Or my future will be guaranteed

Off to the friend garden

Time to weed

Till the soil

And plant the seed

Creating my future

To succeed

Being aware of what I nourish and feed

(Get out the gardening tools!)

THAT

DANG

GANG

THANG

Hector the Projector
Forecasts problems on me
Grumpy - rude - and angry
Is Miss Sour Patch Suzie

Debbie Downer's face
Is always twisted with despair
Plays "wah wah" on the sad trombone
With her depressing flair

Nervous Nellie
She's too scared
Won't leave her house to hang...

Boring Betty
Doesn't show
Much interest in the gang

So there you have it
My five peeps I spend the most time with...
Now I know why I'm down low
That saying's not a myth

We are the sum of all the parts
With whom we spend our time
So raise your bar 'cause
Who you are
Needs those who make you shine!

ANITA

"I NEED A"
MORE LOVE
FOR MYSELF IN LIEU OF
FEAR
SO SEVERE
THAT I MUST STEER CLEAR OF

HONOR THYSELF WITH SELF-LOVE
A SOLUTION THEREOF
NOT A LUXURY
BUT A NECESSITY
IT'S IMPERATIVE HEREOF

A DIVINE LESSON FROM ABOVE
THAT YOUR LACK OF SELF-LOVE
CAUSES ISSUES
NEEDING TISSUES
BY MERE VIRTUE OF

START NOW WITH SELF-LOVE
SO PURE LIKE THE DOVE
ACT LIKE YOUR LIFE
DEPENDS ON IT
BECAUSE IT TRULY DOES

YOU ARE A GEM

You may not see it yet
The truth is yet to find
You're a diamond in the ruff
A precious jewel to be mined

One day the gem will show
When no longer so covert
The elegance and beauty
So well hidden in the dirt

There's no one else quite like you

You are

ONE. OF. A. KIND.

I can't wait for you to see

Your precious stone once it's refined

YOU ARE BEAUTIFUL AND MAGNIFICENT!

TRUST THE GPS

Life is like a drive at night
When it is really dark
You know the destination
On this journey you embark

The headlights on
And off you go
Not seeing
Much ahead
The lights shine on
Just far enough
By a hundred feet
You're led

The GPS will map it out
You only need to see
The next step that's ahead of you
And guided you will be

But if you don't know
Where you're going
How will you know
You're there?
Aimlessly
You'll drive around
And feel that
Life's unfair

It isn't always fair
But you can lower stress and strife
By taking hold and getting in
The driver's seat of life!

THE STRUGGLE...

... IS REAL

Caterpillar
Caterpillar
In your cocoon
You look like you may
Need some help
Hold on I'll be back soon!

I ran inside to get
Some scissors
To help him stop his struggle
It's hard to see
That furry little thing
Look like he's in some trouble….

"I'm back," I cried
I'll get you out
I'm here to save the day"
I cut the cocoon
And out he came
But could not fly away

Oh no what happened
To my friend?
I thought I saved the day
But then I learned a
Sad sad thing
Much to my dismay

The caterpillar
Needs this struggle
To make his wings real strong
If we try to help
In the middle of the fight
He'll never right the wrong

Just like us
When things seem hard
We come out of it
Much stronger
My sweet little caterpillar
Taught me this
So fight the fight no longer

COME OUT OF YOUR SHELL

We should learn from the turtle

Who only makes progress

When he sticks his neck out

Not inside his shell at rest

DARE CONTRAIRE

Don't be afraid to go out on a limb

That's where the fruit is when pickin's seem slim

RHYME TIME

BEDTIME
DREAM TIME
IN BED
I CLIMB

SUBLIME
PRIME TIME
FAVORITE
PASTIME

PLEASE MOM
IT'S TIME
RHYME TIME
STORYTIME!

Oh wait...maybe I should shower first and rid my grime and slime...

THE FOREST OF TRUTH

Once upon a time there was a little acorn seed
He forgot he had within him everything that he would need

With the right conditions - tall he'll grow - from an acorn into a tree
Magnificent with glory - an oak was who he's meant to be

But others started telling him - it's the pine trees that succeed
Deep rooted - strong and flexible - "Be a pine tree!" they would plead

So he tried to be a pine but something didn't feel quite right
Chaos and confusion caused an inner conflict plight

He kind of lost his memory - not remembering who he was
The others may not know him best - but the acorn seed sure does

He finally stopped comparing himself and listening to what they said
So the acorn grew into a beautiful oak - trusting his heart and not his head

SHE'S TRYING TO GO...

Out on the town
In her new ballgown
Mom's trying to get me
To please settle down

I can't calm down
So I jump up and down
Then run around the block
And act like a clown

I'll have a breakdown
If you make me sit down
I need to go play
And swing on the playground

Mom - please don't frown
I just need to calm down
That's why I had to
Run all over town

Now I'll slow down
I'm so tired - worn down
Please fill up the tub
Gee - I hope I don't drown!

OH SHOOT!

From chasing me around
All over town
Mom now has a frown
AND a rip in her gown!

MR. MINIZZLE

I knew a guy named Bizzle Minizzle
He was sharp as a whip
But the Bizzle Minizzle would let out a sizzle
When soda bubbles touched his lip

Bizzle Minizzle and steak with some gristle
Made him freak his freak
The ultra sensitive Bizzle Minizzle
Went berserk when it touched his cheek

Bizzle Minizzle would let out a frizzle
Each time that it would rain
The Bizzle Minizzle did not like the drizzle
It made his skin go insane

So even though dear Mr. Bizzle Minizzle
Was the sharpest tool in the shed
His senses were sensitive to anything he touched
He wished he could just live in his head

Yum Yum

Matzah Brei's
Not made with rye
She said
As she let out a sigh

It's matzah soaked
So it's not dry
Mixed with eggs
Which then you fry

YUM YUM

You should come
Give it a try!

YUM YUM

My senses
Do not lie!
Gotta go
Time to eat
Gotta go... bye-bye!

CRISIS DIVERTED

The word
CRISIS

Seems to brings up fear
But there's another way to view it here

In the Chinese language we're exposed
To the symbols of which CRISIS is composed

They are

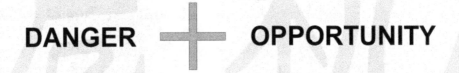

DANGER ➕ OPPORTUNITY

Reflect with hope and unity

Deep thoughts
So next time when crises arise
What traits in you will you comprise?

Scramble up the letters
Make a whole new word
Some are very interesting
The message that's inferred

For example - **DORMITORY**
Equals **DIRTY ROOM**... *hmm*
My son shows this one's true ;)
ASTRONOMER
Equals **MOON STARER**
Yup this one rings true too

Sometimes this fits...
That **CONVERSATION**...
Equals **VOICES RANT ON**
I love this next one
LISTEN equals **SILENT**
Good advice to carry on

THE EYES
Equal **THEY SEE**
A GENTLEMAN - ELEGANT MAN
THE MORSE CODE - HERE COME DOTS
Uncanny although not the plan

SCRAMBLE

JIM MORRISON

A creative genius

He surely broadened the horizon

When he scrambled up his name

And created

The famous **MR MOJO RISIN'**

ONE COOL DANCE MUSICIAN

Oh yes she is

MADONNA LOUISE CICCONE

A very interesting anagram

Since this is how she's known

LAS VEGAS equals **SALVAGES**

STATUE OF LIBERTY - BUILT TO STAY FREE

Could it be true

That **ELVIS** equals **LIVES**

Well then how old would he be?

Not sure - who knows?

If these were created

With intention - wisdom - or blunder

Just have some fun

With anagrams

They're full of wit and wonder

FEEL THE FEELS

I'm excited - sad - and frightened
How can this be?
So many feelings inside of me

Do I have to pick one?
Can't I just feel them all?
All over the map
All my feelings they sprawl

Do I just
Isolate
While I vacillate
Try to
Concentrate
On just one?

Or contemplate
And
Commiserate
While they
Penetrate
I'm stunned

If I try not to feel all my feel-y feel feels
Condemning myself can miss great reveals

I'll stop spinning my wheels
Dig in my heels
Surrender with faith
While I feel all the feels

YOU ARE DYNAMITE

INVITE
DELIGHT
DESPITE
THE TRITE
THAT MIGHT
FRIGHT
AND DIM
YOUR
LIGHT...
IGNITE
THE
FIGHT
OF YOUR
KRYPTONITE
SO YOUR
APPETITE
FOR
INSIGHT
WILL
LIGHT
YOUR
DYNAMITE!

FILTER TILTER

Complaining
Complainers
Wherever they go
Complaints
They bring with them
The outcome we know

The world that they see
Through a lens not so great
No satisfaction
All things aggravate

Not me
No way!
My rose colored glasses
Filter my world
With much LOVE
&
JOY splashes

T R A S H

Garbage in
Garbage out

It's no wonder
So much doubt

Good stuff in
Good stuff out

It's quite simple
BE DEVOUT

CHOICES YOU MAKE
MAKE YOU!

Every choice you make

Leads to the bigger picture

So don't think what you do right now

Will not affect your future

THE RIGHT TRACK

Know what the right track is
Ya know, that middle of the road...
Sometimes you may veer off
Or even come to a crossroad

Get back on - that's what matters
When troubles do confront
Your own moral compass
Should remain in the forefront

Sometimes when at a crossroad
You may not know the way
Be silent and just listen
You won't be led astray

It's no doubt we'll all screw up
No matter how honest and pure
It's your job to stay on track
Or get back on when you detour

So step on up and own it
And learn how to discern
It's how you handle mistakes
And the lessons that you learn

If we only see what we want to see

Maybe it's time to rearrange

Change then what you **WANT** to see

And then what you see **will change**

L O V E
R

F
E
A
R

In every situation
Stop and ask yourself
My dear

"Am I coming from the presence of love
Or the tyranny of fear?"

DOESN'T
EQUATE

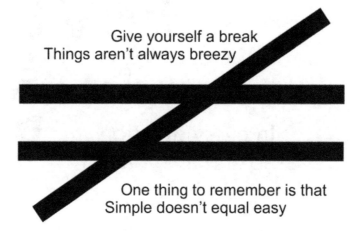

Give yourself a break
Things aren't always breezy

One thing to remember is that
Simple doesn't equal easy

CHOOSE
HAPPINESS

Did you know that

HAPPINESS

Is a choice?

And YOU, my friend, control that voice?

Choose it and life brings all the joys

DO IT NOW

CHIN UP

AND EMBODY IT WITH POISE!

GET OUT OF JAIL

FORGIVENESS

Is like setting a prisoner free

One day I discovered

That the prisoner was me!

Graduates
Patiently await
The great message
The Admiral will spread

He says if you
Want to change the world
Simply start off
By making your bed

If you make your bed
Each morning
You'll accomplish
First task
Of the day

You'll be encouraged
To complete more tasks
Once the first one
Is on it's way

A made bed shows
That little things matter
And gives a small
Sense of pride

It turns a bad day
Into hope for tomorrow
Rest and comfort
It will provide

If you can't do the
Little things right
You won't get
The big ones right either

So make your bed
To create more good
From this habit
That's proven a keeper!

TEACH THEM HOW TO TREAT YOU

You teach people how to treat you
If you put up with their crap they learn
That they can keep doing those things
Even though they may sting and burn

BUT

IF YOU

PUT YOUR FOOT DOWN
&
STAND UP FOR YOURSELF

They'll either stop
Or walk away

Either is better than
The way they were

DO IT NOW

No time for delay!

THERE IS NO LIMIT

Fight for your limitations

And guess what?

They're yours

The sky is not the limit

It's our mind

The guarantors

LOCO

Don't be the loco in locomotive
Be the steam to power the train
Stop waiting for life to happen
And take control of the reign!

ONE DEGREE SHIFT

If you think one degree won't matter
It's time to consider this
A powerful metaphor for life
One you should not dismiss

Water becomes steam at 212 degrees
This vapor can power a train
But it's only hot water when one degree less
A small difference that's quite insane

Hot water itself will not the power the train
It needs just one degree more
Once it turns to vapor and steam
Hear the power of the engine roar!

So be like the water - turn up the heat
And be that extra degree
This is the essence of excellence
Extraordinary results a guarantee

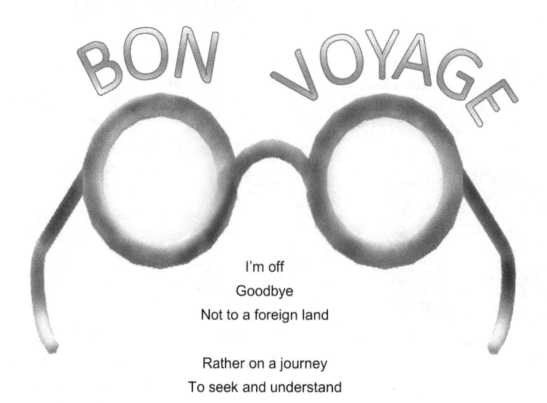

I'm off
Goodbye
Not to a foreign land

Rather on a journey
To seek and understand

Not in new landscapes
Shall I look
It's time to get new eyes

To see the magnificent world anew
Old views are masters of disguise

STICKY SITUATION

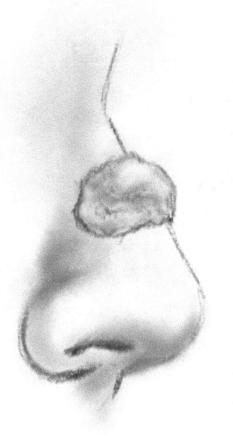

ABC gum

Already **B**een **C**hewed

I find it on the bedpost and the plate
Next to your food
At the bottom of the trash bin which
Doesn't have a bag
So it's stuck onto the plastic now and
Makes me want to gag
It's bright
It's blue
And full of germs
Sometimes stuck to your clothes
If you want to save for later please
Just stick it on your nose

THE
GIFT OF GIVING

Real generosity comes from the spirit
Don't think you don't have it to give
When blessing others with the gift of one's self
You enrich the life that you live

What is a giver of spirit
You ask?
I'll share some ideas with you
KINDNESS & LOVE
PATIENCE & JOY
Just to name a few

You can also bless others
With **TIME** and **ATTENTION**
LISTENING, **TALENT** or **SKILL**
COMPASSION and **WISDOM**
Will go a long way
Or even just **SPACE** to chill

You give *TO* yourself
By giving *OF* yourself
And bless others with the gift of *YOU*
So let the giving begin today
What's something RIGHT NOW that you can do?

YOU ARE
The **GIFT**

Don't bring me a gift
Of material things
The present
Is your presence
Just **YOU** by itself
Is your gift to me

As I'm filled with
The joy
Of your essence

★★
★   ★
★   YOU ARE SUCH A GIFT!   ★
★   ★
★★

THE TENTH
APPLE

There once was a hunter - very well known
Sent on a mission ordered down from the throne

The king wanted this deer - dead or alive
So off went the hunter with arrogance and drive

Deep into the woods to track the deer
He soon lost his way and then started to fear

Hopelessly wandering around in this maze
Couldn't find his way out with no food for 3 days

He thought he'd die of hunger - too depleted to fight
When suddenly an apple tree appeared in his sight!

Delighted and grateful - he started to climb
Collecting many apples to eat for some time

At first he had thought that misfortune had struck
Then marveled at the blessing of his great stroke of luck

He ate the first apple - his joy knew no bounds
Filled with gratitude and joy as he jumped all around

He then became less grateful as he ate the next
And with each passing apple - much less and less

The joy reduced drastically by apple number 10
Complaining and throwing them again and again

How quickly he forgot and went so adrift
He had taken for granted what once was a gift

The 10th apple's as sweet - so don't follow suit
Nothing's wrong with the apple - but the one with the fruit!

FOCUS POCUS

Do things really shift using hocus pocus?
Or is it just an illusion - a **focus pocus**?

Change the focus
Change the perception

Where energy goes
Will get the attention

Could your life be different if you changed the view?
The way you see things and the lens you look through?

Change the focus
Change the perception

Where energy goes
Will get the attention

I'm my own kind of magician - no more hocus pocus!
I choose what I see with newfound **focus pocus**!

JUST WAIT

We will all face tribulations and trials

God's delays are not God's denials

PARDON ME

Forgiving someone

Doesn't excuse

The pain that they impart

Nor does it excuse their actions

It just stops them

From breaking your heart

LET GO OF THE ANCHOR

RESENTMENT
Is like holding an anchor
Then jumping into the sea

You'll drown
If you don't let it go
THE ANCHOR OF ANGER
Is the real enemy

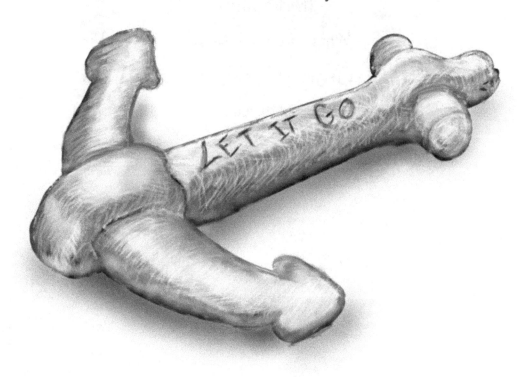

...LET IT GO

FIGHT SONG

Don't be a cry baby

When things get hard

This is exactly

What makes you strong

You get muscle through training

Against resistance

SO RISE UP

And create your fight song!

THE

RISE

The bamboo seed had had enough
Tired of watching his fern friend grow
Brilliant green - fast growing & lush
He wondered why he grew so slow

They both had water - they both had light
The fern grew quickly from the earth
Nothing happened to the bamboo seed
And he started to question his worth

This continued on for five more years
Fern growing with beauty and vibrance
Still. Nothing. The bamboo watched
Depressed as he suffered in silence

Just as the bamboo was about to give up
From the earth came a tiny sprout
And although seemingly insignificant
HOPE now replaced his doubt

The roots had been forming under the ground
It had been growing after all
In six short months this tiny sprout grew
To over 100 feet tall!

The bamboo and the fern discovered
They each had a different purpose
They should never try to compare themselves
Or they won't see what their worth is

Maybe you - too - are just growing roots
The delay is not your demise
You need these roots to grow big and strong
And prepare YOU for YOUR RISE

GOOD
TO THE CORE

Hold the highest standard of integrity
In everything that you do
It means do the right thing
No matter what
Authentic - honest - and true

Nobody may know
Whether you did or did not
But the real test comes from you
At the end of the day
It's you who will know
So ask yourself
How did you do?

Choosing comfort over
Doing what's right
Doesn't do yourself any favors
Stand strong and proud
With integrity
With a character that
Never waivers

A strong moral compass
Plants seeds to achieve
Something we should all strive for
Hold this principle
Close to your heart
It will keep you
GOOD TO THE CORE

THE PEAR TREE

A granddad rocked in his rocking chair - sharing lessons that he learned
The young ones listened intently - as the wheels of their eager minds turned

I sent my four sons - on a quest to observe - just one - single pear tree
Each assigned to a different season - then - report back on what they see

One in winter - One in spring - One summer - One in fall
Until the end - they were not to say - a word - no - nothing at all...

So off they went - to see this tree - that lived a great distance away
Once they're through - they'd gather around - with messages to convey

The first son shared - that the tree he saw - was ugly - bent - and twisted
The second said no - it was green with promise - the first wrong - he insisted

The third said it was laden with blossoms - filled with beauty one couldn't dispute
The last one disagreed with all - describing as ripe and drooping with fruit

The young ones wondered - which was right - all seeming to have good reason
The granddad shared that they ALL were right - for they each just saw one season

Seasons can't be judged - solely by themselves - it's not an accurate view
Rather measured in the end - with a broader scope - once all the seasons are through

Just like the pear tree - we must not let - a bad season ruin the rest
It's who we become - the final blossom in the end - that truly is the test!

(BE PATIENT, YOU WILL BLOSSOM)

C WHAT HAPPENS

Life is

Choices between **B**irth and **D**eath

a.k.a.

C between **B** and **D**

From

Birth to **D**eath

These

Choices add up

Quality of life

Determined by

C

*Every **c**hoice you make leads to the bigger picture.*

*Make **C** count!*

LISTEN TO YOUR MOTHER

Look to the **sun** to fill you up
With an abundance of love and light
The **moon** and **stars** are there for you
To dream with all your might

The **waters** are there to cleanse you
And wash away your fears
The **trees** will always ground you
Growing roots for coming years

The **mountains** will provide you
All the strength you'll ever need
The **flowers** will always bring you joy
But first you must plant the seed

Listen to Mother Nature
As she guides you on your way
All you need is there for you
It's just a thought away

A farmer's horse ran off - and try as he may
He just couldn't catch him - he galloped away
The neighbor looked on - feeling bad for the man
No horse to haul wood - since now off he just ran

Is it bad - is it good? I just don't know
Time will tell - so just go with the flow

The horse came back the next day - with a beautiful mare
He now had two horses - for which he could care
That's great - said the neighbor - *you must be so glad!*
Hmm - he shrugged - *Maybe good - maybe bad…*

Is it good - is it bad? I just don't know
Time will tell - so just go with the flow

When the farmer's son - tried to tame the new mare
He broke both his legs - being thrown in the air
Oh no - thought the neighbor - *It seems I was wrong*
Get rid of that horse - she does not belong!

Is it bad - is it good? I just don't know
Time will tell - so just go with the flow

At the time their country - was going to war
The boy wasn't drafted - which seemed like a score
Broken legs kept him home - with his dad and his cattle
As able-bodied youths - had to march off to battle

Is it good - is it bad, I just don't know
Time will tell - so just go with the flow

This story - you see - does not have an end
Just a great message - to comprehend
Sometimes things that happen - turn out to be good
In the moment - they may just be misunderstood

BACK IT UP

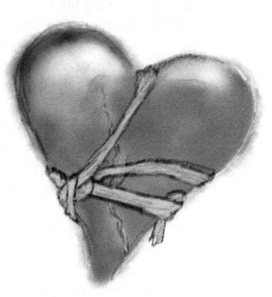

Back it up
You are too close
This love is causing pain
I need a safer distance
To get off this crazy train

I'm backing up
To find the love
Instead of this disdain
Loving from a better place
My heart can still sustain

DON'T
WAIT 'TIL
IT'S
GONE

MOM

FRIENDS

DAD

UNCLE

GRANDPA

SISTER

NEIGHBORS

GRANDMA

AUNT

BROTHER

TEACHER

Appreciate
The PEOPLE
We have in life
Not waiting
To find out
The cost

The VALUE
Of relationships
Are seldom known
That is
Until they are lost

DON'T BE A LOSER

Sometimes ya
WIN

Sometimes ya
LOSE

But please don't get the impression

That if you lose
You failed at it

So Please
DON'T LOSE THE LESSON

LUCKY DUCKY

SOMETIMES NOT GETTING WHAT YOU WANT

IS A WONDERFUL STROKE OF LUCK

**YOU MAY FIND
INSTEAD
IT WASN'T BAD**

**RATHER YOU
WERE
A LUCKY DUCK**

SWALLOW

YOUR

Don't let a little dispute
Ruin a friendship that's great

Swallow your pride

Let it go
&
Make Up

Before it's too late

PRIDE

If you realize you've made a mistake
(Which every one of us will)

Take immediate steps to correct it
(Time makes it harder to clean up the spill)

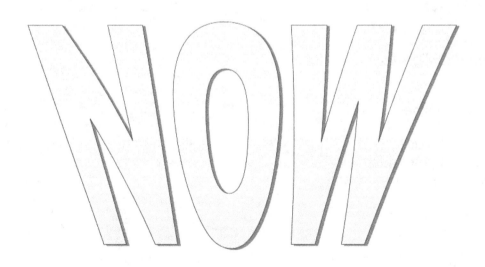

FEATHERS IN THE WIND

Careless words
When tossed about
Can often start a rumor

Even if
Just said in jest

Thought harmless
Just good humor

The victim's name
Now soiled with blame
The words cannot retract

Left hurt and sad
Others may think

Not rumor
But true in fact

Words are like feathers
That fly in the wind
Reaching far and wide

Impossible
Trying to gather back

In the wind
They will reside

Be kind with all
The words you speak
Leave none to misconceive

Trying to gather
Back your words

Is something
You can't achieve

EAT YOUR WORDS

THOUGHTFUL
GENTLE
LOVING
KIND

Keep your words both soft and tender
You may have to eat them tomorrow

They will go down so much easier
Than words causing pain and sorrow

MIRROR
MIRROR

I am BEAUTIFUL

Admiring someone's beauty
Reflects the beauty in you too

You can only see in others
What you already possess in you

TWO HEADS
BETTER THAN ONE

Don't just use all the brains *you* have
Use all of the brains you can borrow

Two heads are always better than one
And can lead to a better tomorrow

Fill your life
With

Understanding
&
Grace

Keeping relationships Civil

By seeing ALL things
Overlooking a bunch
And only correcting a little

We all have an artist
Within to portray

Appreciate the beauty
When on raw display

Whether writing or music
Or canvas or clay

Mediums can come
In a varying array

The medium of LIFE
May be *your artist's way*

As you lead by example
On the path that you lay

Bringing joy and a smile
Uplifting each day

Is an art in itself
A **YOU-nique** art display

HAY, YOU!

Hay, Louise
Thanks for sharing
Your poignant points of view

As you teach in
YOU CAN HEAL YOUR LIFE
For a wonderful life anew

* *We are each responsible for all we experience*
* *Every thought creates our future*

* *The point of power lies in the present moment*
* *Release the past - forgive and suture*

* *Everyone suffers self-hatred and guilt*
* *All think - "I'm not good enough"*

* *But when we truly love ourselves - life works!*
* *IT DOESN'T HAVE TO BE SO TOUGH!*

* *Be willing to learn how to love yourself*
* *Releasing resentment - criticism - and guilt*

* *Thoughts are just thoughts - and can be changed*
* *Self-acceptance (NOW) is how self love's built*

THE WORDS OF THE WISE
THAT THEY SO LOVINGLY SHARE

SAY YOU CAN HEAL YOUR LIFE
AND BE FREE IF YOU DARE

KWIK INSIGHT

If an egg is broken
By an **OUTSIDE** force

Most often that life ends

But if an egg is broken
By an **INSIDE** force

A beautiful life ascends

Time to go within
And find the strength

That in the end will set you free

Working your way
From the **INSIDE OUT**

To be who you were meant to be!

GOOD HABITS

The secret to success lies in
The daily things you do

First **create your habits**

Then your **habits create you**

JUST SAYIN'...

ARE YOU A VICTIM OF YOUR CIRCUMSTANCE?
OR THE MASTER OF YOUR FATE?

YOU CAN'T BE BOTH

so if I were you

CHOOSE

The **MASTER**
&
Create

...JUST SAYIN'

THE
ASCENT

If **THOUGHTS** become **WORDS**
You may need to amend

So words Become **ACTIONS**
You need not defend

How you continue to act
Over and over again
Become daily **HABITS**
Whether or not you intend

As you do these things
Time and again
Your **CHARACTER** is defined
As these habits extend

Your **DESTINY** is determined
By thoughts that ascend

So start with good thoughts
So your life won't descend

KEEP YOUR COOL

Are you more like a THERMOMETER
Reacting to your state?

Or are you like a THERMOSTAT
Which you can regulate?

THERMOMETERS have purpose
Yet just a simple one

Mirroring what's going on
The system is quite dumb

The THERMOSTAT it monitors
Keeps temperature in check

Responding when too hot or cold
With systems to correct

Know how you can self - regulate
Not reacting like a fool

If you lead more like the THERMOSTAT

You will always   KEEP YOUR COOL

Never ever give up hope

No matter how hard it seems

Be
PERSISTENT
&
BELIEVE

In the

BEAUTY of your **DREAMS**

RISKY BUSINESS

RISK it Triscuit was her name
RISK it Triscuit had no shame

RISK of failure comes with trying
Living life is **RISK**ing dying

Live with hope and **RISK** despair
RISK rejection when you care

No **RISK**
Avoids a life of pain

No **RISK** in life
No pain no gain

Safety feels good & may entice
But the cost of freedom has a price

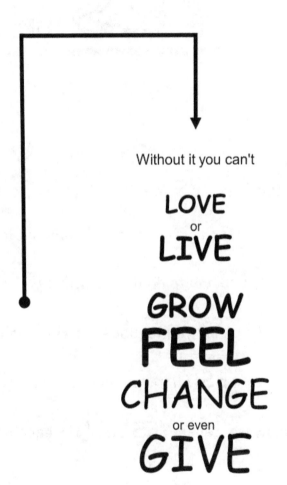

Without it you can't

LOVE
or
LIVE

GROW
FEEL
CHANGE
or even
GIVE

So **RISK** it Triscuit dared to take
RISKs so a great life she'd make

RISK it Triscuit **RISK**ed to be
One who **RISK**s and one who's free

<u>YES</u> or <u>NO</u>

Only say YES to others if you're not saying NO to yourself

People-pleasing meets their needs but leaves yours up on the shelf

It's up to you to do things with NO resentment in your heart

It's ok for you to just say NO - self-advocating is an art

If you say YES when you want to say NO it leaves you feeling bitter

Be aware 'cause YES and NO each have outcomes to consider

DON'T BE

Don't believe

All things you think

Your thoughts may need a tweak

Especially when they make you feel

No good and just plain weak

At times we need to shift things

In our world if there's a kink

But mostly we should go within

It's thoughts that make us shrink

Don't be a shrinky dink

You were meant to e x p a n d!

WAKE UP
WAKE UP

Not of the sleepy kind

WAKE UP
WAKE UP

Awakening of the mind

Don't just follow blindly
Dig deep and you will find
Lots of deep deep truths
Mixed with lies they intertwine

STAY IN YOUR HEART

YOU'RE SMART

STAY IN YOUR HEAD

YOU'RE DEAD

Trust your intuition
To untangle the messy web

It's a very fine art - this dance of life
We must become fine-tuned dancers

All you need is within you now
You've always had all the answers

ASK QUESTIONS

KEEP ASKING
&
THINK
THINK
THINK

QUESTION ALL YOUR THOUGHTS
'TIL THEY FEEL GOOD AND FEEL SUCCINCT

You have it all within you
OH YES YOU DO INDEED!

You were not born to follow my friend

YOU WERE BORN TO  **LEAD**

ORANGE YOU GLAD
I DIDN'T SAY BANANA

The late great Wayne Dyer - had a wonderful way
Of sharing great wisdom - at times done through play

A young man at a lecture - sat in the front row
Wayne asked him a question - he'd seemingly know

He taught us a lesson - at first in disguise
Using an orange as a prop - that would open our eyes

What would come out of this orange - if I squeezed it real hard?
Juice of course - he replied - as this caught him off guard

He then asked him - if apple juice - could possibly come out
He said *no* - as he chuckled - and said *there's no doubt*

When asked - if possible - that the juice was grapefruit
He said *no* - once again - *and there is no dispute*

When asked the final question - regarding the juice
Orange is the only answer - that one can deduce!

Wayne continued to ask - *How come <u>this</u> juice comes out?*
A bit frustrated by now - he even wanted to shout…

…It's an orange - so obviously - that's what is inside!
Wayne then began to share - the great lesson applied

If we assume that this orange - is <u>not</u> an orange... it's <u>you</u>!
When offended by someone - then bad things you spew

They may have squeezed you - and said things - that you didn't like
Then bitterness - or anger - or hatred can spike

Whatever was inside - will come out - as you see...
It's not caused from the outside - like you think it would be

What comes out - when life squeezes - was already there
No matter who squeezes - so we must prepare

Let's fill up with LOVE - not bad feelings - and doubt
So when life squeezes real hard - only goodness comes out!

SWITCH IT CHANGE IT
REARRANGE IT

You may think your stuck in feelings - but what if you apply
A simple way to switch emotions - that we're all run by

To be happy
Let's try this
Hold your head up to the sky

Wear a smile
Even if
It feels like it's a lie

Now really focus on some things - that make you overjoyed
Feel them in your heart so much - that you cannot avoid

Now how about the way you speak - does it bring you down?
If it does
It's time to turn - that negative talk around

We have much more control
You see
Emotions can be changed

Your POSTURE
FOCUS
and
LANGUAGE spoke

Can always be exchanged

HAVE YOU HEARD?

Actions speak louder than words

All for one and one for all

Give him an inch - he'll take a mile…

These sayings I do recall

Early to bed - early to rise - makes a man healthy - wealthy and wise

Don't judge a book by its cover

Measure twice but just cut once

You made your bed now lie in it

He shall find it - he who hunts

Give a man a fish - you feed him for a day - teach a man to fish - he'll have food every day

Absence makes the heart grow fonder

Eat to live - don't live to eat

It's good to give to others

Your needs should not take a backseat

Believe you can and you will

The mind is our greatest limitation

The sincerest form **of** flattery is always imitation

An ounce of prevention is worth **a** pound of cure

Don't make hasty decisions - you'll regret those so much more

You can lead a horse to water but you can't make it drink

And lastly
Don't believe all things - even those you think!

Pain is not *in the facts*
But in the *perception of the facts*

Set your Intention
Trust the Process
Surrender and Relax

Pain opens something up inside
It's what we fill it with that matters

You teach people how to treat you

Follow your heart when it pitter patters

Whatever follows "I AM" will find you
So make those two words count

What you focus on expands
Be aware of where thoughts mount

It's your job to advocate for you
And others to do the same

People show you who they are
Believe them without shame

Intention rules every outcome
Make sure your intentions are good

Trade expectation for appreciation
Then life blossoms as it should

When you know better you do better
So give yourself a break
But don't forget
Your life is based on every choice you make

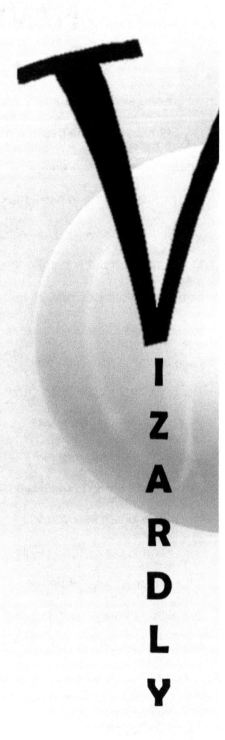

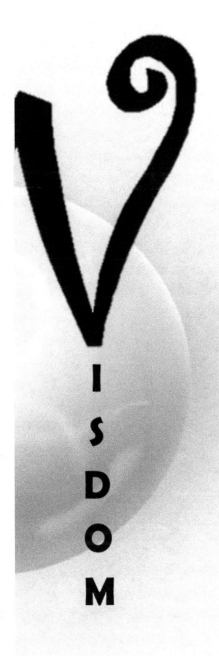

All problems need energy to live

I'd rather be happy than right

The quality of your thoughts
Will equal the quality of your life

Be kind
Be loving
And self-aware
With integrity
As the goal

We were not meant to be perfect
Rather
We were meant to be whole

You are the average of the five people
Of which your time is spent
Rise up
Don't let them bring you down

You're only a victim with consent

Your outer world is a reflection
Of things going on within
If not happy when you're looking out
Let the inner work begin

These are the words of
WIZARDLY WISDOM

If you take to heart and you apply
You can create a life magnificent

And be given the wings to fly!

Alphabetical Index

About the Author

Tracy Hermes resides in the Rockies
Sprinkling the goodness her spirit embodies

Shacked up with her hubby and cute little pup
Empty nesters have left them to fill their own cup

A passionate student of self for some time
She learned many lessons that helped her light shine

Collecting stories, quotes and words of the wise
Helped through many struggles and opened her eyes

Her great love for people and discovery of self
Led to sharing the wisdom that she's found to help

Her humor is quirky, her messages sublime
Direct and made simple in form of a rhyme

She's been a teacher, hair stylist, life coach, now...who knew?
That her poems could be powerful to change your life's view!

CPSIA information can be obtained
at www.ICGtesting.com
Printed in the USA
LVHW011018311220
675398LV00005B/275